[handwritten inscription, partially illegible]

Larry,

To all *[illegible]* years

KEEP PEDALING,
ZEN FARMER

[handwritten text, partially illegible]

Powerlifters in the
Universe. I hope you
enjoy this Book.

Good Luck

Larry *[signature illegible]*

KEEP PEDALING, ZEN FARMER

DORSEY, WRIGHT ESSAYS ON INVESTING

COMPILED BY DORSEY, WRIGHT & ASSOCIATES

AND

JUDD BIASIOTTO, PHD

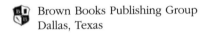 Brown Books Publishing Group
Dallas, Texas

KEEP PEDALING, ZEN FARMER: DORSEY, WRIGHT ESSAYS ON INVESTING
© 2004 Compiled by Dorsey, Wright & Associates and Judd Biasiotto, PhD

Manufactured in the United States of America.

For information, please contact:
Brown Books Publishing Group
16200 North Dallas Parkway, Suite 170
Dallas, Texas 75248
www.brownbooks.com
972-381-0009

ISBN 0-9753907-5-9
LCCN 2004111975
2 3 4 5 6 7 8 9 10

Dedication

A. P. "SKIP" VIRAGH (1941-2003)

As I thought about the topics in this book, such as "Those Who Expect Miracles Perform Miracles," "Self-Confidence," and "Success Is in the Doing, Not the Getting," one person kept coming to mind, and that was the late Skip Viragh. Skip was the founder of Rydex Investments, a truly unique mutual fund company. He was a pioneer in this industry, and his out-of-the-box thinking led to Rydex creating the first inverse mutual fund. This was the first product that allowed an investor to sell the market short, simply by buying a mutual fund, and it filled a niche that had been needed since the inception of the first mutual fund. In essence, he provided the investor another way to employ risk management.

The moment I met Skip Viragh, I knew that both he and I were cut from the same cloth. We both knew in our hearts that the investing public wanted risk management in their portfolios. Skip brought together Rydex and Dorsey, Wright & Associates to create a distinct risk management product, using our methodology and the Rydex mutual funds. Furthermore, he brought this distinct product to Nationwide Insurance Company and the variable annuity product. One man's vision has now extended beyond basic stock market investing and into the insurance industry and will undoubtedly have a positive effect on many investors' retirement accounts. On Wall Street, where just about everything has been seen before, this one man's vision changed the investment landscape forever.

| War | Contentment | Prosperity | Wisdom | Good Fortune | Longevity | Art and Music |

Margaret Ryan has been creating fine art (paintings and ceramics), commercial art, decorative art, and murals for the last thirty years. Ryan comes from a family of artists and studied art at Newcomb College in New Orleans. She has lived in Portland, Maine, for the last eight years. Her murals have been featured in numerous show houses. Contact her at mryan5@maine.rr.com or (207) 871-5934.

The title of this book, "Keep Pedaling, Zen Farmer" comes from the story of the Zen farmer who realizes there are some circumstances in which he cannot control. What he can control are his actions. In life and the financial markets there are many circumstances beyond our control, but what we do have is power over our actions. Changing situations is the one constant in life and in the financial markets, so we must keep pedaling to move forward. Whether the terrain you're pedaling over is rocky or smooth, we hope you find inspiration, guidance, and practical advice from this vignette book.

Table of Contents

Foreword

*W*hat an incredible honor, was all I could think when I returned from a client appointment and saw the e-mail asking if I would write the foreword to a new book on motivation, written by Dorsey, Wright & Associates. That feeling of honor quickly turned to panic. What could I possibly write that would do this book justice?

As I began to reflect on my experience with Dorsey, Wright over the past few years, it all came into focus. At a company meeting in January 2000, I heard for the first time about Point and Figure technical analysis from Tom Dorsey. What he said made sense to me; supply and demand, black and white, and a five-step plan. I could do that. I had become a little skeptical at just using fundamental analysis to tell me what to buy. I definitely needed the part of the equation that explained when to buy and when to sell.

So that day, I went to a local bookstore in Richmond, Virginia, and bought Tom's book, *Point and Figure Charting*, and my money management path was forever changed. From that time on, I spent my time every day reading the *Dorsey, Wright Daily Equity Report*, trying to turn X's and O's into English and eventually into opportunities for my clients. It was great to finally have a method to the madness, to understand that the bottom line in the financial markets was supply and demand.

More significant for me in my reminiscing about my journey with Dorsey, Wright was a doctor's visit in March 2002.

I had finally gotten a spot at the DWA Stock Broker Institute in Richmond. I would be with *all* the analysts from Dorsey, Wright as well as a group of craftsmen from the industry for three days. How exciting! There was a minor detail though. For a few weeks a voice in my head had been suggesting that it might be a good time to go to the doctor. (Who knows, by this time it might have been screaming at me, I had ignored it for so long.) I wasn't feeling "bad," but I wasn't feeling "right" either. The market was not good, I was just beginning to rebuild my own practice, I had clients to take care of, prospects to woo, and an institute to be ready for. Who had time for the doctor?

At 8:30 a.m. on Monday morning, I knew I had a choice— the doctor's office at 9:00 a.m. or the market opening at 9:30 a.m. I chose the doctor's office knowing I needed to take care of "this" now, before the Institute. There was no significant pain, nothing very dramatic, just the nagging of "something is a little off." I was tired and stressed, not sleeping right, not eating right, etc., but at this time I think most brokers were in a similar state. We were feeling challenged by the market and feeling very bad for the clients. By the end of that day I found myself in a semiprivate room at the local hospital, having entered through the emergency room via the doctor's office, and having had full view of the sonogram screen with the large, ominous, unidentified mass taking up most of my belly. THIS WAS NOT ON MY SCHEDULE!

I remember thinking; *how can we get this taken care of so I can go to Richmond?* The short version is that on April 2 I was diagnosed with ovarian cancer. I had canceled my spot at the DWA Broker Institute and was due to be out of work for a month after the surgery (yeah right?!). I remember sending Tom Dorsey an e-mail prior to the surgery to cancel my spot and briefly explaining my plight. I was very upset that I could not attend but looked forward to the next Institute. The e-mail I got back from him said, "Cindy, we're here for you. Let the doctors take care of you now, and we will take care of you later. You are in good hands on both accounts." His e-mail filled my otherwise upside-down world with a sense of relief.

Did I mention that I had met this man maybe once in a room of three hundred people over a year prior? In reality, he had *no* idea who I was other than another broker in another town who happened to belong to another firm who was a client. I was surprised, suspicious, and yet very grateful. I had more faith in him than I did the doctors.

It was a scary time. My health was compromised, the idea of chemotherapy and its effects were uncertain, the markets were *not* doing well, my book of clients was fragile at best, and the pipeline of prospects would slow to a trickle in trying to balance it all. This was not exactly an ideal time to find a salaried job. *Yeah . . . let's hire the bald chick.* I realized that was not an option or a desire. I would focus on what was within my control: my clients and my methodology.

As I look back over old e-mails and *DWA Daily Equity Reports*, I am reminded of this time and clearly see what an impact the whole DWA team had on me as a person and on my survival as a financial advisor. First, they provided me with a simple game plan to manage my clients' wealth. This was not always easy. As I would find, "Chemo Brain" is real. It affects your memory and brain function (not to mention you are pretty much tired all the time). However, I could always go back to my five-step game plan; knowing whether offense or defense was on the field, I'd have a solid idea of what to do. And if I didn't, I would pick up the phone and call Tammy or Sue or Kevin or Paul or Steve or Watson or Jay.

The reports I read every day helped me with a plan to communicate with my clients and prospects. In addition, the message board on their Web site would be invaluable in showing me what other professionals were doing at the time. I also got great support from my own Seal Team One: a group of brokers at my firm, who had attended the DWA Broker Institute, were daily subscribers and generously shared their ideas with me on frequent conference calls.

I think that, most importantly, Dorsey, Wright helped me as a human. Their "motivation" pieces, although I do not know if this was their intent, were *always* a godsend. They showed up on those days when I thought I simply could not do it. I could not pick up the phone one more time. I could not review one more inherited, blown-up account. I could not listen to one more upset client concerned that one more stock that they refused to sell had gone down. And then an article would appear in the daily report, perhaps a letter from another broker talking about helping a client, and the DWA perspective of how many people really needed our help. And I would think, *I can do that! That is what I am here for!* Sure, sitting at home puking my bald head off is probably an option, but not today. Maybe I will consider that tomorrow. Today, there is someone else who wants to retire someday, who wants to leave a legacy to their children, and they need to hear about an alternative to buy, hold, and hope. That there is offense and defense in the stock market and that *cash* is an investment sometimes.

One particular article that I remember reading was entitled "Choking: Tips for Controlling the Terror of Coming Unglued," with paragraph titles: Putting Things in Perspective, Don't Be Afraid to Make a Mistake, Be Prepared, Focus on the Moment, Develop a Consistent Behavioral Pattern, Look at the Worst-Case Scenario *(Excuse me? Am I not living it?)*, and Look for the Silver Lining in each Situation. Now, I am sure when most brokers/clients read this article they related it to the market conditions of 2002. I, however, got to see it from a few different angles. My world had come unglued, and I had the opportunity to stop and put things in perspective—like I had a choice. Tom and company helped me do this every day. Sometimes it was via the articles, and sometimes it was from a phone call about my current game plan, reassuring me that I was still on-target. Always, it was from a team of caring professionals without whom I would not have survived that summer.

There were days when the chemo would have its way with me and begin to win the fight for my body. And usually on those days, there would be an article about being GREAT and what it took to be exceptional at your chosen profession. I would devour those pieces and regain my focus on helping my clients and anyone who would listen, having great faith that I had that ability and obligation to help—sometimes just lacking the physical strength to do so.

I had my last chemotherapy that summer 2002, and as I sat in the chemo room I got a call from my assistant telling me that a foundation, which I had been working on for a year, had finally signed the paperwork. I had landed my largest account! My first call was to Tom Dorsey to celebrate and to thank him for all his help in keeping my head above water, and for showing me a methodology that would make sense to people and would help them protect, preserve, and build their wealth.

I am now cancer free and Tom Dorsey, his associates, and his clientele are still showing up when I need them most and expect them least. Just last week I was asked to present to the board of a bank. In watching the indicators, the financial sector had begun to deteriorate. My timing of the presentation was great, but just how should I put that information into a logical format? Just days later, right there in the report, was a great outline for a presentation on the technical change in the banking sector. Once again DWA to the rescue!

As I have said many times over the past few years, I do not know that I would be in this business if I had not been introduced to Point and Figure Technical Analysis by Tom Dorsey. I am always curious how other brokers survived the bear market and how their discussions with their clients went during that time. I feel I am very blessed to have a game plan that I understand, I am excited about, and that I can use effectively to manage my clients' wealth. Most importantly, I have an incredible team of professionals beside me at all times.

So, to you the reader, I hope that you will find inspiration, support, thoughtfulness, and motivation in this book. I know you will find the passion coming through the words of the people of Dorsey, Wright. May you use it to fulfill your destiny.

To Dorsey, Wright & Associates: Thank you!

Thank you, Tom, for picking up A. W. Cohen's book oh so long ago, for finding your passion and your light, and for raising that torch high enough so that others may follow. Thank you for shining it brightly to illuminate the incredible team you have built around you.

To the other DWA clients, thank you for sharing parts of yourselves through your e-mails, through your successes shared in the daily report, and through your messages on the board. They do make a difference.

And especially to *all* of the DWA team, you may never know the role you played in my survival, not only from cancer but also from an ever-challenging stock market. I am eternally indebted for always providing an answer to the questions whether I asked them or not, for making me laugh when I wanted to cry, for methodically walking me through the steps when I couldn't see straight, and for always being there when I needed you.

Thank you for helping me to survive during my fight and thrive during my life.

With great gratitude,
Cindy Hamill

Preface

How do you preface a book like this? There are so many people involved in writing it. Dr. Judd Biasiotto, a sports physiologist and college professor, is a co-author of this book. I guess he's had the greatest influence on me, when it comes to motivational writing. Judd and I have a long history together that began before I even had the pleasure of meeting him. I have been reading Judd's motivational writings in *Powerlifting USA Magazine* for many years. It's my favorite magazine by far, and Judd is the main reason. Oh sure, I love all the muscle stories and new techniques for lifting massive weight, but the articles that have had the greatest effect on me have been Judd's motivational writings. We, first and foremost, are connected through lifting weights. Both Judd and I have been world record holders in the sport of power lifting. Judd had to leave the sport after breaking his back while performing a massive squat. True to form, however, he came back, not in power lifting, but in the sport of bodybuilding. In his fifties, Judd won many national championships, beating bodybuilders much younger than he. Much of what he has written has motivated me to push on to achieve my own world records.

Every time I read an article by Judd, I thought how closely his sports analogies applied to the stock brokerage business. I called Judd and asked whether he minded if I reworked his articles by intertwining my thoughts on the brokerage business. It was kind of a strange endeavor, weaving two authors' independent thoughts into one article, but he was all for it. The articles were to be free-flowing; that is, we would not stop after each paragraph to let the reader know who wrote it. We just let our words meld together as one article, like combining oil and vinegar to make a salad dressing. The first article we did engendered such a positive response from our clients that I knew we were onto something. Most importantly, we got our points across and had fun doing it.

I also invited Judd to speak at our annual Stockbroker Institute one year where he was a smash hit. You see, Judd is also a world-class speaker. But what really sets him apart from others is his love and care for people. For example, he called me one day and asked if I would help him raise money to buy a specially-fitted van, suitable for a quadriplegic named Kenny. Kenny had become paralyzed in a motorcycle accident and was virtually a prisoner in his house, with no transportation. I said I'd surely help. Judd was writing a book about Kenny, and the proceeds were going toward the purchase of this van. I relayed this story to my wonderful clients through our daily research report, and the money poured in. More people than you can imagine rallied around this cause, and you know what? Kenny is driving his van now, thanks to Judd. The van released him from his prison of immobility. The people who helped in this project are too numerous to mention in such a short space, but they were all godsends.

Judd is truly a Renaissance man. In addition to teaching college classes, being a world-class bodybuilder, and helping others, he has written over forty books. They range from instruction on abdominal workouts to motivational books.

The lessons I have learned from Judd proved invaluable during a recent experience I had. I was asked to speak at the convocation for the James River High School senior class located in Richmond, Virginia. The governor had been the school's first choice for speaker, but he was unable to attend because of a prior commitment. Somehow my name came up as a possible replacement for him. I was dumbfounded. I would be a replacement for the governor? No way! But, Carson Raymond, senior class president, called and asked me to consider being the keynote speaker for this event. I was surprised, to say the least. Although I have spoken all over the world for decades, my audience has never been high school seniors. I speak on the stock market, technical analysis, managing portfolios, and succeeding as a Wall Street professional. Because I was honored, I immediately accepted the speaking engagement at James River High School. But after I accepted, as I thought about it for a few minutes, I broke out in a cold sweat.

The thought of speaking for thirty minutes to a group of eighteen-year-olds was very unsettling to say the least. What in the world would I tell them? After some deliberation I decided to simply tell my life story. I thought it might resonate with some of those high school seniors. Since this book is about motivation, it might help to learn a little about how desperately I needed motivation at one time in my life.

Growing up, I had a very difficult time in school. I have been in sixteen different schools in my life, some for as short as six months. In addition to having attention deficit disorder (ADD), I was somewhat dyslexic, and at age fourteen I totally gave up on myself. I decided the only path for me was to become a professional bowler. It may sound funny, but I had an innate ability to bowl well, and that was in the era of bowling. It took me an extra year to graduate from high school and, true to form, I promptly flunked out of a junior college my first semester.

Vietnam was in full swing and Uncle Sam was not interested in my desire to bowl professionally. If you were not in college with at least a C average, the military was your next stop. I chose the Navy. It took four years in the Navy to change my attitude, and now I'm on Wall Street. There is more to the story—including overcoming alcoholism—but that is for another time and another book. Toward the end of my speech to those high school seniors, I began to discuss some motivational topics that Judd and I had written about over the years. I finished with some simple ideas on how to become successful in life. At the end of my talk, those seniors gave me a standing ovation. It brought tears to my eyes. I was not prepared for such a response. Apparently something I said resonated with the whole senior class. Something motivated them to action. You will read some of that speech in this book. I hope it resonates with you. This book is a compilation of that speech and other essays and articles that honor our collective history.

As in our daily research report, we do not point out who writes which article in this book. We often get requests to note who wrote a particular article, but we have always refrained from doing that. The reason is we have a team approach at Dorsey, Wright. It's the team that puts out the daily research, not one person, and oftentimes more than one person works on an article.

This book is also a team effort. Tammy DeRosier is a contributing writer of the book. Tammy has been with me since she was sixteen years old. I'm not kidding! She has been with Dorsey, Wright since her high school days. She is now in her thirties and my "right hand" at DWA. She writes every day for our research report, and Judd's writings have touched her, too. Some of the conversations we have in this office early in the morning eating breakfast are often the springboard for many of the motivational pieces Tammy writes in the daily report. Those pieces are also included in this book.

Paul Keeton is another one of my analysts who contributes to the report each day. Paul has a natural knack for setting the perfect stage. You almost feel like you are in an Alfred Hitchcock movie when you read his pieces. An avid fan of all sports, Keeton relates sports back to the investing world in many of his writings. Along those lines, my partner Watson Wright is an avid golfer, so some of his writings pertain to golf. Watson and I started Dorsey, Wright & Associates in 1987. We had no clients, had borrowed money, and had given up stable positions at Wheat First Securities. All we had was hope and a prayer. Seventeen years later, we're still standing and looking forward to the next challenging decade. We have been able to accrue the best group of people one could possibly hope to have in a company during these years.

Other key writers for this book are Susan Morrison, Kevin DePew, and Jay Ball. Susan has been here from the beginning and is instrumental in our daily research. Kevin DePew is one of our newer analysts, having joined us in 2000. Kevin was a broker before he came to Dorsey, Wright, so he brings a current perspective on being a broker. You will also find some writings from Jay

Ball, who heads up our Internet Technology Department. What makes Jay so unique is that he is also an analyst, so anything that is added to the Web site goes through the eyes of an analyst, not just a computer programmer. And that also keeps the DWA Internet system as useful as it can be for you, our end user.

Dr. Judd was the inspiration to write this book and he, along with other influences, continues to inspire us. One of our biggest inspirations is our loyal, dedicated, hardworking clientele. During a time of corporate malfeasance, analyst corruption, and mutual fund scandals, it is inspiring to know that there is an army of stockbrokers and Wall Street professionals out there striving to be the best they can be, all for the good of their clients. Our greatest satisfaction comes in knowing that we've been able to touch the lives of so many investors in America through the craftsmanship of their brokers, who truly understand the concepts of both wealth accumulation and wealth preservation.

This book is meant to be ultimately accommodative. You can read it from start to finish, or open it and randomly select a piece to read each day. However you decide to read this book, we hope you enjoy it. Above all, we hope it makes a difference in your life.

Setting Goals:
The Power of Purpose

Judd Biasiotto at the weight of 132 pounds, squatted 605 pounds for a world record. This feat of strength remains unsurpassed to this day. He's definitely been an inspiration to me in my power lifting endeavors, and much of his motivational writing has helped me attain heights I never thought possible. I was able to attain an Amateur Athletic Union (AAU) world record in the dead lift for the fifty to fifty-four age group, even though I didn't start lifting weights until I was forty-seven years old. It all kind of happened by accident.

I remember my first meet. I didn't even know I was required to wear a wrestling singlet to comply with the regulations for AAU power lifting. I learned what real sportsmanship was at that meet. One of the other lifters offered to loan me his singlet after each of his lifts. I mean, I went into the men's room and changed from my shorts to his singlet and back after each lift. I'll never forget that act of kindness and sportsmanship. I remember this person at every meet I attend, and if anyone ever needs any help whatsoever, I'm there to give it, thanks to this person who unselfishly helped me. Boy, what one act of kindness can do for a person! You know, this

> **Goals are essential to success. Without goals there is no direction, no hope, no growth. Every human being must have a purpose in his life just to stay alive.**

is the only sport I know of where age is a benefit. The older you get, the less competition there is. I think most lifters are burned out by the time they reach their mid-fifties, so since I started so late in life, I haven't had time to ruin my joints yet.

I have been successful in the sport of power lifting by setting small, attainable goals. I guess that holds true for my whole life. Over the years I have found many similarities between world-class power lifters and world-class investors. At Dorsey, Wright we are devoted to helping you attain world-class status for both individuals and professional investors. In a recent article in *Powerlifting USA Magazine*, Dr. Judd Biasiotto discussed how he retired from lifting in 1983 because he had more or less lost his direction as an athlete. He would still go to the gym to work out, but his enthusiasm had waned. He explained, "My heart just wasn't in it. I didn't have any clear-cut goal or purpose for training. Consequently, I stumbled through my workouts, never really knowing where I was going and never really getting anywhere. My workouts had no intensity and I had no drive or desire. Take my word for it—not having a goal is the worst thing that can happen to an athlete or anyone else for that matter. Goals are essential to success. Without goals there is no direction, no hope, no growth. Every human being must have a purpose in his life just to stay alive."

I experienced the same feelings Judd expressed when I was a stockbroker in the 1970s. I really had no goals each day other than to generate production. It was a constant scramble to do business. The idea was simply to get as many clients as we could by cold calling and generate as much production as possible from it. This made the branch manager happy, and we would all have a better life. Production did come, but growth did not. I have seen many brokers leave the business because their hearts just weren't in it. They had no goal and, as Judd had done, simply stumbled through each day without having a direction. Individual investors are the same way. They stumble through half-hearted investment strategies and eventually give up; when it is all there for the taking. How many of you stumble through each day, with no clear-cut goal or purpose for being in your particular job? Look around you. How many people do you know who come to work each day totally unprepared? Look around you and count them. You might be surprised.

To truly succeed in any business, including the business of investing, you must have purpose. You must have something

When you lose purpose in what you're doing, you become a lost soul.

you look forward to accomplishing. When you lose purpose in what you're doing, you become a lost soul. I believe this was never more evident than with Mike Tyson, the former heavyweight champion of the world. When Tyson first turned pro his goal was to become the greatest heavyweight champion ever. That goal was extremely important to Tyson. In fact, that's the only thing he ever talked about or, for that matter, ever thought about. It was his sole purpose in life. That one goal kept Tyson on track. He sacrificed everything for it. He didn't drink, didn't date, and wouldn't even leave his training camp. All he did was train. He was totally driven toward achieving his goal. In the ring, he was relentless, a madman. He would beat his opponents from one end of the ring to the other. Some of the beatings he dished out were merciless.

When Tyson claimed the Heavyweight Championship of the World at twenty-one, he was already considered the greatest champion of all time. Here's where he began his downfall. Instead of looking forward to further growth, he looked at immediate gratification. That spelled the beginning of the end for Tyson. He remained on the defensive, always trying to defend his present position instead of going on the offensive and trying to attain new goals. He started going out at night in pursuit of the things he had previously avoided. He slacked off on his training. And then do you know what happened? An average fighter by the name of Buster Douglas knocked him out. It was one of the greatest upsets in the history of boxing. I watched it. When Buster Douglas was interviewed after the fight, do you know what he said? "My sole purpose in life these last six months was

> # Goals are not just visions. They are visions that are acted upon.

to beat Tyson. That's all I thought about. He was the first thing on my mind when I woke up in the morning and the last thing on my mind when I went to bed. When I'd fall asleep, I would dream about beating him. If there was anything else going on in the world I didn't know about it because my mind had just one thing on it—beating Tyson." After that fight, Douglas faded into obscurity as did Mike Tyson. Tyson tried several more times to capture the crown and eventually was mercilessly beaten by Lennox Lewis in their championship fight. Many of you in your own profession might find yourself in the equivalent of Tyson's position. It's not too late to change and put your focus back to where it needs to be.

Goals are not just visions. They are visions that are acted upon. Unlike Tyson, once you meet your initial goal, don't stop there. At Dorsey, Wright we continue to meet goals and then strive for others. It's the journey we love at DWA. The goals we attain here are merely stepping-stones to a never-ending quest to maintain our world-class status. As an investor you should also continue striving to achieve or maintain your world-class status. Every positive outcome we experience is an ultimate triumph for our goal-driven hard work and will create further ambition for what we have yet to do. Once we are truly able to believe and have confidence in our goals, our inner abilities, and ourselves, the sky's the limit. The key phrase is *confidence in your abilities*. This comes from study and hard work. But once you have confidence, your potential is limitless. I have told my children that college is simply a stepping-stone. What college will do is teach you to find the answer and give you confidence that you can do anything you choose to do. The rest comes from the heart.

To develop a systematic, goal-oriented program try the following steps:

1 First, set goals that are realistic and flexible. Don't set your goals so high that you ensure failure. Don't set a goal of a three-hundred-pound bench press in four months, when you are only a two-hundred-pound bencher now. Unrealistic goals will lead to frustration and, eventually, failure. Conversely, don't set your goals too low. Keep your goals just out of reach, not out of sight.

2 Develop a hierarchy of goals. Put each goal in writing. Establish primary, secondary, and long-term goals. In the gym, my long-term goal is to capture the Raw Masters Bench Press World Record. I was able to attain the World Record for the Dead Lift. I did not quit there. I focused on my next goal. Each week in the gym I set a small goal to accomplish. My goals are short-term, small and incremental, but ultimately lead to long-term: Raw Masters Bench Press World Record.

3   List obstacles to achieving each goal. Often, achieving your goals will include a number of other considerations. If you are an investor, obstacles may include lack of time to study the art of investing because of family requirements, children's school, sports, etc.

4   Identify the resources that can help you. This list might include your spouse, parents, books, and institutions of education. Also, getting in shape physically might take you a long way toward achieving each goal.

5   Construct a game plan. Be sure to put it in writing.

6   Act on that plan. Remember, merely writing down a goal does not guarantee that you will achieve it. As we mentioned, goals are more than just visions—they are visions being acted upon.

You Gotta Keep Pedaling the Bicycle to Move Forward

To act without clear understanding,
to form habits without investigation,
to follow a path all one's life
without knowing where it really leads,
such is the behavior of the multitude.

—Mencius (371–288 BC)

To act without clear understanding of technical analysis
and the economics of supply and demand,
to form habits in investing without investigating exactly what you are doing,
to follow a path all your investment life
without having a solid, logical, organized plan for investing,
such is the behavior of the multitude of investment advisors.

—Tom Dorsey (1947 to present)

After doing a presentation on our methodology, we see the lights go on in people's minds, and it's a great feeling to know you've educated someone. They're excited and ready to go because they've been introduced to a new way of looking at the markets in a logical, sensible, organized manner that allows them to manage risk in their accounts. Inevitably I'll get the question, "Why isn't everyone doing this?" or "Will this become a self-fulfilling prophecy?" The answer to both of these questions is that it takes work to master the methodology, and it takes work to continue using it.

> **You have to keep pedaling the bicycle if you want to stay on.**

I was talking to one of our most astute clients who told me that he and his associates had been teaching younger brokers the methods of successful investing; they included DWA's Point & Figure methodology. One broker approached my client and said, "Boy, this is a lot of work." He responded to the broker, "That's why they call it 'going to work' each day." In other words, you have to keep pedaling the bicycle if you want to stay on. Managing risk in your accounts is a never-ending process. The markets are always ebbing and flowing, and if you decide to stop pedaling, you're going to fall off. There are times when the surface is relatively flat; we can coast along, and pedaling is pretty easy. This happpened during the 1995 to 2000 markets.

There are other times in which we have to pedal pretty hard to keep our balance, as in the 2000 to 2003 markets. But those who can grit it out and keep the bike steady on those hard slopes ultimately come out on top.

Buy and hold is always the path of least resistance. That doesn't make it the best path, though. It is all about when you get on the investment train. If you got on in 1929, it took you twenty-five years to get back to even. That's a steep hill to climb. If you got on the investment train in 1973, that was another time with a pretty steep terrain; it took you 7.6 years to get back to even. If you got on the investment train in 1982, it was pretty easy pedaling.

For so much of the wealth today, investors had enjoyed pretty easy investing terrain until the year 2000. The potholes and tough terrain came on with a vengeance. Performing in line with the S&P 500 has brought investors' portfolios back to 1997 levels. At an 11 percent per year return, it's going to take you a little over five years to get back to even. Again, that's *if* the market returns 11 percent per year from the 2002 lows. If the market averages a 1 percent per year compounded return, like the Dow Jones did from 1965 to 1982 (not including dividends), it is going to take you fifty-seven years to get back to the 2000 highs. That figure does not even factor in inflation.

I received a call from an investor who had signed up for a trial subscription to our DWA research report. He said he had been on trial about two years ago, but had "fallen off the train," so to speak. He found that too much work was required to have to make changes in his accounts when the indica-

> **There really isn't any way to be a risk manager and not take an active role in reviewing the accounts.**

tors changed risk levels, so he stopped using the methodology and went back to the "buy and hold" philosophy. But that hasn't worked either. He wanted to know if there was a way to buy quality companies and hold those without having to implement the changes in the indicators or take the time and effort to review the portfolio's positions on an ongoing basis. My response was, no, there really isn't any way to be a risk manager and not take an active role in reviewing the accounts. According to the book *Creative Destruction*, only seventy-four of the original five hundred stocks in the S&P 500 in 1957 remained on the list in 1997 and only twelve of those survivors had outperformed the index. Reviewing positions is an ongoing process that never stops.

We've also taken several calls and e-mails from investors who have said, "This is really a tough game, especially when the markets don't go straight up." They are exactly right. When the pitches are coming down the middle of the plate, we have to be ready to swing. Sometimes we will pop out, sometimes we'll hit a home run, but most of the time we'll hit a lot of singles. Over the course of time, hitting a lot of singles will make the portfolio quite successful. The "grinding it out every day" is what adds up in the long run.

I was talking with our money managers the other day and Mike Moody made a good point about the DWA Money Management philosophy. We are always there gritting it out day after day, in the up markets, the down markets, and the sideways markets. Our money managers are the guys at the gym who are there January 2, February 2, March 2, December 2—all throughout the year.

The Art of Winning:
How Failure Teaches Us

The story of Thomas Edison's life is a prime example of the American dream. Without question, he was a giant among men. He saw light when others saw darkness. During his lifetime, his patents, a record 1,093 inventions, literally revolutionized the world. He was truly one of the greatest minds in history. However, Edison also knew failure. In fact, he failed quite a bit. But like all great men, Edison looked at failure as a learning experience—an experience that would help him grow and develop. His first patent, when he was all but penniless, was for an electric vote-recorder, but maneuver-minded legislators refused to buy it. At one time, he had his entire fortune tied up in machinery for a magnetic separation device for low-grade iron ore. That machinery became obsolete and impractical by the opening of the iron-rich Mesabi Range. But Edison never stopped inventing new ideas when he feared failure. "Shucks," he told a discouraged co-worker during one trying series of experiments. "We haven't failed. We now know a thousand things that won't work, so we're that much closer to finding what will."

> **It's amazing how fast you find your way when you accept responsibility for your actions and, in so doing, accept success or failure on its own terms.**

I had to fail many times as a broker and investor before I finally found my way. I didn't know how to become excellent at investing. I always thought that the key to investing was simply doing what my firm told me to do, and if I lost money for a client, it was the analyst's fault. Only when I was given the opportunity and responsibility to develop and manage the first Options Strategy Department at a large regional firm did I realize that the key to success resided within me and I had no one else to blame. I had to become the one responsible for my recommendations and research. There was no passing the buck—the buck stopped with me. I was prepared to live or die by my recommendations.

It's amazing how fast you find your way when you accept responsibility for your actions and, in so doing, accept success or failure on its own terms. This is when the Point & Figure method of stock market analysis came to light for me. Before I opened myself up to other possibilities in the stock market advisory business, I found every way imaginable to fail in my duties as an advisor. I guess I was kind of like Edison. I found thousands of things that did not work on Wall Street before I found something that did. It was there all the time, and schools teach it every day in Economics 101: supply and demand.

After a fire had destroyed his whole laboratory, Edison said, "You can always make capital out of disaster. We've just cleaned out a bunch of old rubbish. We'll build bigger and better on the ruins." It's obvious that Edison did not view his setbacks as a hindrance. Have you lost money in the market and failed to learn from that mistake? Or have you taken the time to evaluate just what went wrong and to take the necessary steps to correct it?

If you learn from your mistakes, you become a much better investor. If you blame the fundamental analyst for the stock going down, you are not taking responsibility. Conversely, if the stock does well, it's also your call. In the three years from 2000 to 2002 there were seven trillion dollars lost in the market. That's seven trillion. Can you imagine what a trillion dollars is? Most people think that million, billion, trillion is just an arithmetic progression, from one to two to three. One million dollars is a stack of thousand-dollar bills eight inches high. A billion dollars is a stack of thousand-dollar bills six hundred feet high. A trillion dollars is a stack of thousand dollar bills 2.3 miles high. In the years 2000 to 2002, there were 16.1 miles of thousand dollar bills, stacked end to end, lost in the market. Has anyone learned from this devastating loss to America's investors? I fear not.

I have seen so many brokers and investors give up after this kind of bear market. They probably gave up, because they all fell into Alan Greenspan's "irrational exuberance" comment. But Edison didn't give up after the fire. At 5:30 the next morning, with the fire barely under control, he called his employees together and announced he was rebuilding. Edison told one man to lease all the machine shops in the area. Another, to obtain a wrecking crane from the Erie Railroad. Then Edison proferred, "Oh, by the way, anybody know where we can get some money?"

A new age is upon us. Do you need to begin planning now to restructure your investment process like Edison did following the fire at his laboratory? If you are a professional in the investment business, do you need to rebuild your relationships with investors? Or as an investor, do you need to change your relationships with the particular advisors you deal with? If your advisor is not performing, do like we do in Virginia with hunting dogs that just ain't hunting. We trade them on trade date. Are you going to simply begin another year on the wrong foot? Maybe there is nothing that needs to be done but if there is, get on it now!

Failure teaches us. Or, to quote Ben Franklin, "Those things that hurt, instruct." If we get burned, we learn not to play with matches. If we make a mistake, we learn not to do it again. Nobody—whether you are a professional or an individual—can

> **It's how we deal with the occasional, inevitable failure in investing that determines how good we will ultimately be as investors.**

avoid failure all the time, especially in the investment business. Investing in some way is a part of our lives. Failure will always be part of the landscape. It's how we deal with the occasional, inevitable failure in investing that determines how good we will ultimately be as investors. If you continue to make the same mistakes over and over again you are doomed to failure.

Bob Dunwoody, a world-class motivational speaker for investors, says, "The definition of insanity is doing the same thing over and over again—expecting a different outcome each time." One way to make sure you don't do the same thing over and over again is to actually write down why you buy a particular stock. If it turns out to be the wrong decision, you can easily go back and evaluate just what went wrong. As you learn from your mistakes, your confidence will rise. Losing is more instructive and informational than winning. For instance, research has revealed that athletes have a greater tendency to analyze their performances when they lose rather than when they win. Of course, when an athlete's performance is analyzed, mistakes are brought to the forefront to be examined and corrected. Terry Bradshaw of the Pittsburgh Steelers, two-time Super Bowl MVP and Hall of Famer, once said, "Failure is the most critical element to success. I don't know of a single great athlete who hasn't tasted defeat. Until you're beaten, victory has no meaning."

If your stock picks or portfolio management results fall short of success, don't blame others. Take full responsibility for your behavior. A person who takes total responsibility for his shortcomings is usually admired. Don't just accept your mistakes—learn from them. Analyze why you failed in your

17

investment performance. You might have to fire an advisor, but you must fire them if they are not performing. Face it, the only reason you invest any money at all is to make more money. You send out a dollar and hope it brings back a dime. Forget investing for the long term. We don't have "long term," as many investors have learned over the last few years. We have the here and now. Never look out past your headlights. This way, you always keep everything in focus. Don't ever accept any lame excuses for consistently poor performance. Remember, "This Is Your Life." Also, remember that everyone fails in the investment process at some point or another. Failure is part of being human. I have talked to many investors who just couldn't get it right. They were on the verge of totally giving up until they analyzed what was going wrong in their stock management process and finally got it right. In many cases, the only requirement is to embrace technical analysis along with unbiased, solid research. Stop, think, evaluate, and make adjustments. You can be great. Success is simply the manipulation of error.

A Time for Truth

When I attended a military institution of higher learning for four years, I appreciated the brutal honesty of it all. When I heard the phrase (and I heard this one often), "Cadet, you're gonna learn to fear me like your worst nightmare," it was typically not far from the truth. I was frequently reminded exactly how slow I was on morning runs, exactly how poorly shined my shoes were at any given time, and exactly how much my grades looked like a decent batting average rather than a decent GPA. For a stretch, these admonitions were completely accurate, but at some point any person would grow weary of hearing such unflattering accusations and equating them with the truth. Logically speaking, the most direct way for a person to change his or her situation would be to perform more favorably, thus rendering the accusations false. In my case, this was a heavy workload, and sometimes life sends a few extra crates of lemons your way.

At some stage in the game, facing reality was a necessary step for me to take. It was not the easy step, mind you. It would have been much easier to find some quick fix for the problem, otherwise known as an excuse. If my shoes weren't shined, it's because I didn't have time. Not fast enough at this morning's run? Not a problem. I stayed up too late trying to write a paper that would better my batting average. See, an excuse is always available as a quick fix to any problem. *Yes, I know my portfolio is down for the thirteenth quarter in a row. But, I'm a long-term-oriented investor, and I can't be shaken by short-term fluctuations in the marketplace.* See how that works? We have a problem, and then we quickly follow it up with a short-term fix or excuse.

In my case, I realized that my first semester GPA was unsustainable; even if it was a batting average, it would have caused me to be sent down to the Minor Leagues via a Greyhound bus. I could probably create excuses for the situation, but no amount of excuses was going to produce a diploma. The short-term fixes were never going to help me meet my long-term objectives, and it was clear to me that the easy way was not the right way. Similarly, these excuses will rarely provide for an investor's retirement, and so they do nothing to help the investor reach his or her long-term objectives.

Worthless idioms are simply no longer accepted. The average investor didn't think the market could go down three years in a row. Telling the average investor that there is no twenty-year stretch in history that would have left any investor in negative territory is just as useless, primarily because the average investor doesn't have twenty years. He surely doesn't have twenty years to risk being fully invested in equities just to try to recoup what he has already lost. The time for excuses and empty idioms is over. The time for truth is here.

The truth is that 75 percent of the wealth in America is held by those fifty years of age or older, and those are not long-term-oriented investors. Their grandchildren may be long-term investors. The truth is that if you invested $100 in the Dow on the first trading day in 1929, it was worth less than $20 by the last day of trading in 1932. The truth is that while we haven't had many stretches where the market is lower ten calendar years later, we have had seventeen of them since 1896. The truth is that if you bought at the top of the 1929 market, it took you twenty-five years to get back to even. And the truth is that the Dow Jones Industrial Average has returned not 11 percent and not 12 percent, but an average of 7.04 percent annually since 1896. That's the truth, and while it hurts, it gives us something to work with.

We can accept these aspects of investing history, or we can make excuses for them. Excuses are short-term Band-Aids. What investors need right now is the truth. There are ways to manage risk in this market, so just throwing our hands up and continuing to subscribe to the buy and hold philosophy simply isn't the answer for most investors. The truth may hurt, but it may also set us free. Excuses will do little in the long run.

Careful Where You Get Your Zen

CBS Marketwatch commentator Paul Farrell published an article entitled, "Politics Replaces Rational Investing, Wise Zen Farmer's Story Offers a Solution," which featured the well-known story of the Zen farmer and his horse. Here is the story, if you do not already know it.

Story of the Zen Farmer

A farmer's horse disappears one day. His neighbors, noticing the horse is missing, gather at the farmer's house one evening after farming and remark upon his terrible luck. The Zen farmer shrugs and simply says, "We'll see."

The next day the horse returns and brings with it several wild horses that the farmer can use to speed up his plowing in the field. The neighbors gather once again and remark on his good fortune. The Zen farmer shrugs and says, "We'll see."

The following day the farmer's son is thrown while trying to ride the horse and breaks his leg. The neighbors again gather and offer their sympathy and condolences for his mis-

What is, is.

fortune. Again, the Zen farmer shrugs and says, "We'll see."

The day after his son breaks his leg, officers from the Emperor's Army arrive to seize all able-bodied young men in the village for mandatory service. The neighbors gather to commiserate and tell the farmer how fortunate he is that his son recently broke his leg and was therefore spared from the soldiers. Again, the Zen farmer shrugs and says, "We'll see."

The wisdom of the Zen farmer is that we can never know just where the winds of fortune will blow, how they will chart their course, or, ultimately, how they will affect our future. Nevertheless, we don't throw our hands up in defeat and refuse to farm. We adjust our expectations, make certain we are using the best farm implements we can find, and go to the fields every day knowing that we are neither masters of our fate, nor victims of it; instead, we are students.

At Dorsey, Wright we often say, "What is, is," a view very closely related to the Zen farmer's "We'll see." Where many people see defeat and hopelessness in this view, we see something altogether different—something positive and calming in the fact that we are very aware of that which we cannot know. While the Zen farmer's neighbors are content to ride the roller coaster of fortune's highs and lows, often overestimating their own role in bringing them about, the Zen farmer is at peace with the fact that whatever fortune may bring, good or bad, he plays no role in its whims.

> ## The craftsman has the tools to deal with the unknowable aspects of the market.

Similarly, those of you who are craftsmen in the Point & Figure Methodology understand that we are powerless to alter the course of the financial markets. Frequently, we do not even comprehend why they move the way they do. For example, who thought the markets would ever rise again following September 11, 2001? Who thought the markets could rise as we entered war with Iraq in March of 2003? The craftsman is content to accept that which he does not know because he has a set of tools to guide him through the good and bad of the markets. In other words, the craftsman has the tools to deal with the unknowable aspects of the market.

The Zen farmer isn't necessarily better than his neighbors; he's just better at focusing on the things he can change and ignoring the things he cannot. Similarly, the craftsman is better at focusing on the things he can change about a portfolio, such as the risk profile and the market exposure, and ignoring the things he cannot, such as what the Fed does with interest rates or, more dramatically, what the accountants at WorldCom and Enron do.

The Power of Belief

I'm convinced that the power of the mind is God's greatest gift to us. I'm also convinced that the secret to unlocking that power lies in belief. Belief, I contend, is the magic elixir that can transform a mediocre athlete into a world-class competitor.

The same transformation can happen for an investor. I talked to an investor not long ago, who called to tell me his investment success had changed dramatically since he embraced the Point & Figure methodology and had subscribed to *Value Line*. His portfolio is actually up in the worst bear market I have seen in twenty-eight years on Wall Street. His confidence has doubled because he now believes in himself and his abilities to make money and manage risk in his own account. The word *belief* is

Confidence is key to the ability to act rather than react to changes in the marketplace.

so powerful—it's life-transforming. Confidence comes from education and experience. Confidence is key to the ability to act, rather than react, to changes in the marketplace.

Throughout my years of competing in sports on a world level, I have used a formula for success. It goes like this: *Conceive, Believe, and Achieve.* It's simple, but profound. I'm sure most of you have conceived of yourself as being great at one time or another. I believe that's very important. When I was a little boy I always saw myself as being AWESOME. In fact, I was always visualizing myself kicking Larry Holmes's butt or breaking Hank Aaron's home run record. I never had a problem conjuring up images of myself doing something spectacular. The problem was that, in my heart, I really didn't believe I could reach such heights. There is a big difference in conceiving yourself as being great and actually believing that you are going to be great.

When I grew up, I used to think about those things, but the delusions got even bigger. Back in the '70s, I thought of myself as some sort of great option trader, worthy of a statue being erected on Wall Street. Well, maybe not that grandiose, but a big statue nonetheless. It didn't take long for the market to teach me a lesson I would never forget. It's like being regressed back to the mean. Once you begin to get too far outside the tails of the bell curve, life has a way of snapping you back to the center. I had confused my brain power with a bull market.

Bull markets are a kind of *Twilight Zone*, where investors and brokers alike have visions of greatness backed up with virtually nothing. Now that I have abided twenty-nine years in this business, the last thing I want to be is some sort of great trader.

I am far more interested in amassing wealth than experiencing the satisfaction of scalping a small profit. I have met many an investor who thought he was great during the bull market, but once the bull market was over, so were his investments.

Back in the Internet/technology bubble, most investors began believing the investment process was easy. You just bought the stock of Red Hat at $287 a share and watched it go up 30 percent in a week. It's the same way investors used to act in the 1500s during the tulip bubble craze in Holland. In 1962, the American market went through a bubble just like the Internet/technology bubble that burst in 2000. That time it was aerospace. Even bowling supply stocks went through the roof at one time, until someone calculated that every man, woman, and child in America would have to spend five hours a day in a bowling alley to support the swollen prices of those stocks. Optimism soon turned to pessimism and the down move was on. It has been said that wherever there is a bubble, a pin is not far away. Nothing has changed since the first recorded market bubble in Holland over five hundred years ago. Fear and greed continue to dominate most investors' emotions when it comes to investing. And it will happen again, just like clockwork. Maybe not for another decade, but it will happen. It has been said that bear markets return money to their rightful owners.

It's when you truly believe you can be great (and that you are going to be great), that you are close to being great. Your goals are within reach. At that point, you have the vision of how to arrive at that goal. Belief is the power that transforms mediocrity into excellence. Believing in yourself opens the doors

> **Belief is the power that transforms mediocrity into excellence.**

for success. The consequences of that posture are that you don't know what heights you can hit—the sky is virtually the limit. Belief, however, must be backed up with knowledge and experience before the success part of the equation can materialize. So just believing you can break the world record for bench press is unrealistic unless you visit the gym on a regular basis and implement a solid, logical, organized plan of attack. The same goes for investors, both professional and individual. Greatness comes only through study and application. It takes time to walk around the block a few times.

I love the story about the chicken and the eagle. It's an old Indian fable about a young brave who took an egg from an eagle's nest and put it into a chicken's nest. When the egg hatched, the baby eagle thought he was a chicken. As the eagle grew up among the chickens, he learned their way of life. He pecked the ground for food, scratched the dust, and made vocal sounds like the chickens he lived with. One day he looked into the sky and saw an eagle soaring above him. He flexed his wings and said to his mother, "I wish I could fly like that." "Don't be silly," his mother said. "You're a chicken, only eagles can soar so high in the sky." Feeling foolish and convinced that his desire to fly was futile, the eagle went back to scratching and pecking in the dirt. He had, for

> **Although our perceptions of reality determine what we believe, what we believe determines who we are and what we will become.**

all practical purposes, become a chicken because he believed he was a chicken. Never again did he question his role on earth.

It is all a matter of perception. When the eagle couldn't fly, it wasn't because he didn't have the natural ability, but rather because his belief was, *I am a chicken, and chickens can't fly.* In order to fly, he needed to alter his perception of himself. He had to recognize his God-given abilities and/or change his mindset concerning these abilities. He had to believe in himself. Although our perceptions of reality determine what we believe, what we believe determines who we are and what we will become.

If we perceive ourselves as traders, like those in the movie *Wall Street*, then that is the type of investor we will become. I know this because I've been down that road. What I'd really rather be, however, is someone who accumulates wealth. That requires working at a logical, organized, disciplined approach that recognizes the need to buy and sell. It also means that a slow and steady approach is best suited to gain wealth because risk is managed along the way.

As human beings, we tend to act according to what we believe is true, regardless of what is actually true or false. In other words, we are the product of conditioning in much the same manner that a computer is the product of its programming.

For seventeen years now at DWA, I have seen brokers and investors transformed from chickens to eagles. I once was a chicken when I was a stockbroker. There is no worse feeling than coming to work each day and being afraid of which customer will be the next one to lose money due to the next great recommendation from my firm. The feeling of being out of control permeates your thoughts. You never have enough of the best stocks you own, and you always have too many of the worst. You sit at your desk afraid the phone will ring and a client will ask you what you like. You look at the calendar and become painfully aware that the end of production for the month is drawing near. So you go into survival mode and produce. You become acutely aware that you are a chicken in an eagle's world, but you don't know how to become an eagle. These feelings build and eventually you give up and change your business from taking control of your clients' accounts to giving control to others to manage. You settle for chicken status, giving up on the chance to fly in your career. How many people in your profession are settling for chicken status? Are you one of those?

Others I see envision becoming an eagle and they go for it. They realize that they can't do it with their current knowledge, so they do whatever it takes to obtain the knowledge required. We have numerous individual investors I would put up against most money managers on Wall Street. They have soared to eagle status because they believed they could. Knowledge is power, and as they gain more knowledge, they gain more confidence and believe they will become an eagle. This confidence and belief are contagious, and people want to follow those who are confident. Money under the management of confident advisors expands; the success ratio on their investments also increases significantly. They are on their way to soaring.

The transformation in my life from chicken to eagle happened when I read the first paragraph of the introduction to the book *The Three Box Reversal to Point & Figure Technical Analysis* by A. W. Cohen. I came to the realization that, as a broker at a large brokerage firm, I had only half the equation to work with—only the fundamentals. Fundamentals answer the question of what to buy; but technicals, which are equally important, answer the question about when to buy and sell. One without the other is like playing the piano with only one hand. Overnight I soared like an eagle. I had become reacquainted with the IRREFUTABLE LAW OF SUPPLY AND DEMAND. A simple economic law that I had studied at my university for four years hit home the second time around. I had transformed myself at that moment from chicken to eagle, and my transformation led to the development of Dorsey, Wright & Associates. I have seen it happen with brokers and investors time and again. When it comes to Wall Street, I would say we at Dorsey, Wright have more eagles as clients, both professional and individual, than any other firm. What type of bird do you want to be in your career?

Tips for Better Golf and Better Business

One of my habits, which may or may not be very good, is letting magazines pile up. There's always an article of interest in just about everything I read, and I want to keep them for reference. Eventually, I end up with a pile of magazines taller than my 5-foot 2-inch frame. At that point I know I must go through my magazine file and do some sorting. While sorting through magazines recently, I came across an article by Dr. Robert J. Rotella. He was the director of sports psychology at the University of Virginia and currently acts as a consultant to many professional golfers and writes extensively about golf. In this particular article he offers ten tips for playing golf. But really, these tips are for life in general. I thought they were worthy enough to reprint here and to discuss how they pertain to being an investor.

1 **A person with great dreams can achieve great things. I am a firm believer that if you set the standard low, the achievement level will be low. Set your sights high. Don't underestimate yourself.**

Reading *Point & Figure Charting, 2nd Edition* by Tom Dorsey and charting a couple of stocks by hand each day is a great accomplishment. Complete the DWA Global Online University and push yourself even further. We are a nation, a world, on information overload. Don't underestimate your abilities to become an expert at managing risk in the stock market.

2 There is no such thing as a golfer playing over his head. A hot streak is simply a glimpse of a golfer's potential.

So you've picked a couple of winners in a row. What did you do to pick those stocks? You probably didn't choose them based on the office gossip about the next possible takeover candidate. Those winners were probably the result of hard work. They were the result of solid research during which you stuck to a game plan.

3 It is more important to be decisive than to be correct when preparing to play any golf shot, particularly a putt.

Life on Wall Street means that you will not be correct every time. However, you must not let that fact keep you from sticking to your game plan. One of the problems with pursuing perfection is hunting for the perfect method. Trying a new system each week will not get you to your goal. To get there, you must remain focused on one method and maintain consistency and discipline. You may find that Fibonacci numbers, Gann angles, or astrology works for you, and that is fine. But, once you find a method that you are comfortable with, you must stick with it.

4 **Golf is played by human beings. Therefore, it is a game of mistakes. Successful golfers know how to respond to mistakes.**

It is okay to be wrong in a trade, but it is not okay to stay wrong. If you are going to take a road trip from Richmond, Virginia, to San Francisco, California, one of the first things you do is get a map. If there is an accident along the way that shuts down the highway, you can pull out your map and find an alternate route. It is the same way in investing. You must have a road map for investing. As you know, every trade is not going to be perfect, but often your portfolio is successful, not because of what you own, but because of what you don't own. Respond to mistakes. It is always easier to address the successes rather than the failures, but failures need the most attention. If you don't address the failures, then you will soon have a portfolio of clunkers. Learn to fail fast.

5

On the first tee, a golfer must expect only two things of himself: to have fun and to focus his mind on every shot.

Life is too short not to have a good time. If you come to the office in the morning and sit down at your desk dreading the rest of your day, then you should take a good hard look at whether you want to be in that particular business or not. The Internet has leveled the playing field in so many businesses. It is more important than ever that you embrace your profession with enthusiasm, competitiveness, and more knowledge than ever.

The truly successful brokers, or anyone for that matter, are people who genuinely enjoy what they do. Every day is a new, exciting challenge. When you have a game plan, it makes all the difference in the world. You know whether to have the offensive or defensive team on the field. Imagine being a football coach and the referee tells you to put a team on the field. Imagine that once both sides have a team on the field, the referee arbitrarily gives one team the ball. It would be really tough to play a great game. It's the same way with the stock market. Imagine trying to make a decision not knowing whether you are playing offense or defense. If you don't have a game plan, it makes investing really tough and takes the enjoyment out of it.

6

The quality of a golfer's practice is more important than the quantity, especially for the better golfers.

When there are so many financial products available, it's easy to throw up your hands and just not make a decision. There are ways to get this behemoth of products down to a quantity that is manageable and to which you can devote some quality research. In fact, did you know that the top 120 capitalized stocks in the S&P 500 account for about 80 percent of the movement in that index? Maybe those 120 companies are the inventory you work from. Or maybe you narrow it to local companies, focus on Exchange Traded Funds (ETFs), or pick a family or two of mutual funds. Be sure to limit your inventory to products for which you can spend some quality research time.

7 **Golfers must learn to love the challenge when they hit a ball into the rough, trees, or sand. The alternatives— anger, whining, and cheating—do no good.**

Investors must also learn to love the challenge. Anyone can buy a stock; it's the true craftsman who knows how to manage that stock position once it's in the portfolio. Some of the best discussions on the DWA Bulletin Board have been about managing both winning and losing positions once they are in the portfolio.

8 **To score consistently, a golfer must think consistently. A consistent pre-shot routine makes it easier.**

This goes back to sticking with a plan that you believe

in. It's easy to get sidetracked if a trade doesn't work, but you must maintain consistency. Switching to a new plan each week will not get you to your goal. Find something that you believe in and stick to it. Knowing your game plan like the back of your hand makes it easier to function in any kind of market.

9. The loss of focus on four or five shots per round makes the difference between great golf and mediocre golf.

Let's face it. Losing focus can be easy to do when managing money, especially if you don't have a game plan. Money is fraught with emotions. Listening to the news media only amplifies those emotions. When the market is rallying, the mood is one of euphoria; it's easy to get swept up in that and put positions into the portfolio that your game plan would not have otherwise told you to do. Conversely, when the market is dropping sharply, it's easy to feel like "throwing the baby out with the bath water." You lose sight of the fact that strong relative strength stocks may break down, yet make higher bottoms than the market, and are often the first to come back once the market gets back on solid footing.

10. Courage is a necessary quality in all champions. But an athlete cannot be courageous without first being afraid.

Investors need a good dose of respect for the market. It is a formidable opponent.

Self-Confidence

Self-confidence is a word that really says it all. Have it and the world is yours. Be devoid of it and mediocrity is likely to be your high point. In the business of investing, it's an essential ingredient to success. To have self-confidence is to have some method that defines your existence. Webster defines confidence as: "firm belief; trust; reliance." It is the act of being or feeling certain, having assurance, believing in your own abilities, relying on your own powers. Self-confidence transcends more than the business of investing. It's the key to success in all of our endeavors. A great athlete first and foremost believes in himself. The most consistent finding in sports-related research is the direct relationship between self-confidence and success. Research has

> To have self-confidence is
> to have some method that
> defines your existence.

consistently shown that athletes who are confident think and act significantly different from athletes who lack confidence. Just look around your office. Who is a confident broker and who isn't? The confident ones stand out. The confident investor acts significantly different from an investor who is not confident. When I was a broker, the brokers in our office who had no confidence were always blaming someone else for a stock's decline. They never assessed what their own abilities were to evaluate a particular stock before recommending it to a client. Wayne Dyer said it best about placing blame on others:

All blame is a waste of time. No matter how much fault you find with another, and regardless of how much you blame him, it will not change you. The only thing blame does is to keep the focus off you when you are looking for external reasons to explain your unhappiness or frustration. You may succeed in making another feel guilty about something by blaming him, but you won't succeed in changing whatever it is about you that is making you unhappy.

I talked to a branch manager not long ago, who related a private discussion he had had with a broker in his office. The manager had advised the broker that, to succeed in this business, he needed to embrace some method to build confidence in his abilities to manage clients' assets. The broker thought about it for a while and, instead of doing what was necessary to increase his abilities in this business, he tendered his resignation. He had no confidence in his abilities and was unwilling to do what it took to gain this confidence. In my opinion, he did the right thing. He is probably in another business that is more suited to his abilities.

Athletes who are confident believe they can do anything—and often do. They never quit; they constantly see themselves as winners, never losers. If you look at the Larry Birds, Michael Jordans, and the Steffi Grafs, you'll see people who have a powerful belief in their skills and in themselves. These are people who can create magic and work miracles. For example, in Evander Holyfield's first fight with Mike Tyson, Holyfield was a 45-to-1 underdog. While Tyson had been beating up every one of his opponents mercilessly, Evander had been having trouble with his fights and physical trouble with his heart. But the 45-to-1 odds didn't faze Holyfield one bit. He had confidence in himself. In the pre-fight interview he guaranteed that he would win the fight. He said, "That's a promise. I know in my heart I will beat Tyson!" Well, you know what happened. He knocked Tyson out in the eleventh round. It was one of the biggest surprises in boxing history. It documented what courage, determination, and self-belief can do.

Holyfield is only one athlete who has transcended a performance level that was thought to be his peak. Just remember Joe Namath, Muhammad Ali, Buster Douglas, Monica Seles, Greg Louganis, Dan O'Brien, Carey Struthers, Walt Disney, Bill Gates, Lee Iacocca, Donald Trump, Oprah Winfrey, and Arnold Schwarzenegger, all of whom made the seemingly impossible possible through the power of belief. I could name numerous stockbrokers who had been on the brink of resignation but finally found their way and are now top producers for their customers and their firms. These professionals have made miraculous turnarounds. In my book, *Thriving as a Broker in the 21st Century,* I describe Scott Bowers, who made a similar turnaround. His branch manager was going to fire him and he called Scott into his office to deliver the bad news. Scott jumped in with the old adage about how investors often make the mistake of selling stocks out at the bottom when the news looks the darkest. He told his manager that he was about to sell him out at the bottom. His manager bought that analogy and gave him another chance. His job was saved and he turned out to be one of the best brokers I know, as well as a top producer for his firm. He had confidence in himself and knew he was ready for a turnaround—in fact, he had a major breakout!

The magic of believing applies not only to physical performances but also to every aspect of human behavior. Our actions, feelings, and abilities are consistent with our conditioning and/or programming. In short, we tend to "act like" the type of person we perceive ourselves to be. Not only that, but we literally cannot act otherwise, even if we make a conscious effort to do so.

Obviously, then, the way your brain has been programmed will go a long way toward determining how successful you'll be in the stock market business, in athletics, and in life. The Navy Seal teams are the epitome of physical and mental conditioning. Their tremendous success in some of the most difficult battle conditions is a testament to their training. Do you think that, when a team of Seals are dropped in the dead of night behind enemy lines, and out-manned 100 to 1, they have the slightest thought that they won't be successful? They eat, sleep, drink, and act like the greatest fighting force known to man, and they continue to prove that they are. How would your office fare, if employees were as mentally and physically trained and conditioned in your business as the Seals are trained? I can tell you what would happen. You would have an office of workers who exude confidence and ability. The office would comprise a close-knit group, operating in an all-for-one and one-for-all atmosphere. They would operate as a team, with the well-being of clients and their firms first and foremost in mind. Clients would be attracted to them like magnets.

Did you know that George Herring was only seven years old when he told his parents he was going to be the strongest man in the world? Cassius Clay was only eight years old when he told his mother he would one day become the heavyweight champion of the world. Neil Armstrong was ten when he told his dad he was going to be a famous aviator. And here is something that is absolutely incredible: In 1985, while performing in small comedy clubs for minimum wage, Jim Carrey wrote himself a check for ten million dollars for services rendered and dated it 1995. And you know what? The day before Thanksgiving, 1995, Carrey signed a movie contract for, you guessed it, ten million dollars.

It's interesting to note that some of the greatest achievements in sports and life as a whole were performed by people who didn't realize that what they did was impossible. Men with vision, men who believe are the men who rule the world.

> # Nothing is impossible if you
> # believe in yourself.

Let's be honest; we all have voices in our heads that undermine our faith in our abilities. They make it easy for us to blame others for our shortcomings. We have to work on trading in those negative voices for supportive, more realistic ones. As I said earlier, nothing is impossible if you believe in yourself. The greatest dreams that have been accomplished by men and women have been called impossibilities, but they proved that the impossible was possible. Confidence is contagious. It doesn't happen by accident and certainly not overnight. It takes time and devotion to become a true craftsman in this methodology of investing. Once you reach that level you will know it. Your competition will become virtually nonexistent. Remember, through belief you can do or become anything you desire. You can go to the stars. Just put your mind to it and watch the magic unfold.

The Importance of Focus

I believe an important factor in achieving success is the ability to live in the moment, to focus all of your energies on the task you are performing. Webster's dictionary has one of the definitions for focus as "the ability to fix or settle on one thing; to concentrate." Boy, that definition hits home! I had to revisit a university for a second time to realize that when a professor said to read a chapter, he meant to retain it, too. You know, that sounds so funny, but many of our youngsters today don't grasp that concept. I remember in school telling my mother that I did what the teacher told me to do: I read the chapter. Unfortunately I still failed the test. The teacher did not say, "Read the chapter and by the way, while you are reading it, I'd like you to be thinking about playing baseball."

I still have to remind myself to focus when I read an article or a book. I also find that the more I work at it, the better I get. You know how I learned to read and retain? I had to stop after each paragraph I read and ask myself what I remembered from that paragraph. If the answer was nothing because I was not focusing on the task at hand, I chose to read it again. Soon

> **If you learn to become totally consumed with every task that you perform, you can produce amazing results.**

my mind was so tired of reading and re-reading, it automatically began to focus on the task of reading and comprehending. It was the only way I could reach college-level reading. I guess if schools had been able to test kids when I was growing up, I would have been diagnosed with ADD. I don't know how much that diagnosis would have helped me. I just had to eventually find my own way. You know something else? Once I began to read and retain, I started to enjoy reading for the first time in my life.

When you are totally focused, you can submerge yourself completely into whatever you are trying to accomplish. And once you are capable of doing that, you can make something extraordinary happen. When nothing exists except the game (or the task you are engaged in), then you can perform at a higher level. Some athletes refer to this as being "in the zone." In business, medicine, or the stock market, it is referred to as "the white moment." During this time, nothing seems beyond the boundaries of possibility. Your stock selection and management of portfolios seem peerless.

The secret to success in anything is to keep your mind focused on the thing you want to accomplish. If you learn to become totally consumed with every task that you perform, you can produce amazing results. Think about how much unfocused time you spend each day. How many co-workers come into your office just to shoot the breeze? How often do these co-workers break your concentration? I remember that interruptions were constant when I was a broker. I was still easily distracted at that point in my life. To bring about the best results, you must be completely preoccupied with the here and now. When I wrote my first book, I sat at a table for hours on end, writing and thinking. Before I knew it, a day had evaporated. Writing a book became a single-minded focus for me. One page led to a chapter, and chapters led to a book. This led to the second edition of that book, then another and another, and here I sit focused on completing this book. My English teachers would never believe it. Heck, nobody who used to know me would believe it. Actually, keeping a single-minded focus is the way I approach everything I do. I give my undivided attention and my greatest effort to whatever I'm doing at the time. If I'm writing, I write. If I'm lifting weights, I lift weights. If I'm talking, I talk. If I'm reading, I read. And if I'm playing, I play. I try to capture the essence of the moment, because once it is gone, it is gone forever.

The story of Carlos Kleiber, the magnificent symphony conductor, is a prime example of the power of focus. Kleiber was concentrating so intently when conducting at La Scala, the famous opera house in Milan, Italy, that he was unaware that an earthquake was shaking the entire building. A giant chandelier directly over his head was rattling so violently that many people in the audience got up and ran, screaming, out of the auditorium. Even some of the members of the orchestra got up and ran out. Amazingly, Kleiber never reacted to the commotion until one of the orchestra members informed him that the building was on the verge of collapsing. He was able to shut out the extraneous stimuli and, at the same time, synchronize the forces of his mind and body in order to conduct his symphony. Interestingly, the term *genius* has been described as "the ability to focus on one thing at a time." That definition certainly applies here. Of course, other performers, such as athletes, surgeons, artists, writers, musicians, and investors, can also achieve this kind of focus.

Now is the only time over which we really have control. We need to perform every act as if nothing else in the world matters. This is an old Zen principle: you put your whole soul and being into every act that you perform. Arnold Schwarzenegger was a master at this type of concentrated training when he was competing in bodybuilding. He centralized his total body energy into the muscle he was training. (He may have to call on this skill as governor of California.) Be that as it may, let me share what he says about focusing on the moment and/or the task at hand. He says:

> *When I trained, the most important thing was that my mind was always in touch with my body. That not only helped my training, it was like meditating. I could get into myself. I locked my mind into the muscle during training, as if I transplanted my mind into the tissue itself. I became one with the weights. Nothing else in the world mattered to me.*

> **Only the immediate moment has significance; for it is only that moment that you can control.**

When you think of it, the only reality in life is what is transpiring now—what is happening with us at this very moment in time. That is what is important. Think about it. What has occurred moments before is irrelevant, as is what might happen in the moments to come. Only the immediate moment has significance, for it is only that moment that you can control.

In investing, we tend to worry too much about what might happen. We are barraged with research reports about what might happen in the future. When we are investing with sacred money, we tend to focus on what might happen if the stock doesn't work. We fret about the possible earnings' shortfall or the product acceptance in the future. We overlook what the stock is telling us right now. We really have nothing else concrete to go with. Focusing means being totally in the here and now, as in John Lennon's words, "Life is what is happening while we are reminiscing about the past or contemplating the future." Many investors today spend too much time thinking about the past or the future. But the stock market is speaking volumes to us each and every day in the here and now.

One of the things that total focus does is eliminate fear and anxiety. Those are two words we live with in investing or any business. On the one hand, lapses in concentration invite fear and uncertainty. Consider what would happen if I asked you to walk across a board that was twelve inches wide, fifteen feet long, and a foot off the ground. I'm sure you would be able to complete that task without any difficulty. In fact, you could probably do it blindfolded. On the other hand, what if I extended the board between two New York skyscrapers with a drop of about one hundred feet to the ground? I would be willing to bet that a walk across that same board would cause considerable anxiety for you. I'm sure that some people would simply not be able to do it. The skill level required to walk across the board is exactly the same, whether the board is twelve inches or one hundred feet off the ground. The difference is in the psychological response to the perceived risk. Instead of totally focusing on the task, your attention is directed to the possibility of what could happen. Many brokers and investors freeze up when it comes to buying stocks because, instead of focusing on what is, they focus on what might be.

This type of lapse in concentration occurs often in sports. Field goal kickers who are near perfect in practice from a short range miss "chip shots" in game situations when the pressure is on. Basketball players shoot a brick on a simple foul shot when the game is on the line. Why? Lack of focus. They are thinking more about the outcome than they are about employing their skills.

Obviously, staying totally focused on the task at hand is a significant mental edge, a skill if you will, that can help you elevate your performance in every aspect of your life. Such control does not come easily nor can it be learned through a haphazard effort. It takes time and discipline, but it can be learned. Once you've obtained the skill, you can become immersed in each situation that you encounter. Each moment will be infused with importance and necessity. When you reach that point, you can go beyond what you even think is possible, so begin now to focus on your daily tasks.

March Madness...
Life Is Sport

I f there ever could have been a year when you finally thought, for once, that we could move gracefully through the Ides of March without so much as an utterance concerning "UNC," it should have been 2002. And then came the upset of the first round, where the USC Trojans fell to whom? None other than your UNC Wilmington fighting Seahawks! It may not have been UNC Chapel Hill, but it was definitely too close for me. Nonetheless, as I watched my South Regional bracket come apart like a Firestone radial, I found solace in knowing that there are other endeavors in which I excel.

The amazing thing about the financial business (and we should all thank God for this each and every morning) is that you don't have to be able to dunk a basketball to win at it. You don't have to run a 4.4-second 40-yard dash and you don't have to be able to bench-press a Volkswagen either. It might help to have a name like Michael Vick, but you don't need his left arm or his legs to be successful. With my innate ability to attain mediocrity in just about any sport from an early age, I count this realization as quite a blessing. Growing up, I was always good enough to start on the varsity sports team but never quite good enough to score the goals. The coaches always showered me with phrases, such as "great effort" or better yet "good eye," which can be candidly transposed to "Oooh, not quite," and "Thank goodness, you didn't swing at that one," respectively. These were hardly the same idioms I heard Marv Albert use in reference to Michael Jordan or Joe Montana. So I did not accept my shortcomings gracefully.

Perhaps the most painful reality was that my deficiencies did not result from lack of effort, which was never the issue. I just wasn't gifted at the particular endeavors I chose. It took a long time, and more than a few lessons in physics, to learn the mechanics of how one person may run a five-minute mile with relative ease, while a stubby country boy from rural Virginia may take that long to lace his shoes. I learned, eventually, that we can all be successful at something, but we can't all be successful at something like basketball or long-distance running. (When I say "we," I mean we stubby country boys from rural Virginia. I am relatively sure anyone else on the face of this earth has a good chance at playing basketball on the NBA level.)

Life sure would have been easier if all sports were like skydiving or bullfighting, where you find out very quickly if you are any good or not. But often that isn't the case. Most of us spend our formative years stumbling over soccer balls and cowering in front of approaching ground balls before realizing that we are gifted at some unrelated activity. Nonetheless, it is this mutual experience that makes sports a common language for us all.

At Dorsey, Wright, we often make references to sports in our writings, but not because we expect all of our readers to be avid sports fans. We rely more squarely on the power of sports to help communicate our thoughts concerning the market. When we say, "The NYSE bullish percent just reversed into bear alert status at 64 percent," we are speaking to a handful of people who understand the concepts and methodology. When we say that we are "playing defense," we are speaking to anyone who has ever missed a ground ball or was goofing with the bees, as a simple pop-up sailed past, which unsheathed the facetious phrase "nice defense" from a coach or loved one. Whether through prior success or spectacular failure, we can all relate to sports in some aspect. Not only that, but we know in our heart of hearts that the same rules for winning in the sports world apply to winning in life and business alike.

Time and time again we find similar patterns of success for those who excel at sports and those who excel in other walks of life. I was reading an article in *Newsweek* last year that reinforced this concept. They had interviewed many athletic champions: Michael Jordan, Tiger Woods, Wayne Gretzky, Jackie Joyner-Kersee, and Joe Montana, to name a few. The attributes found in these individuals who have clearly succeeded in their sports also exist in successful stockbrokers, money managers, and investors we talk to each and every day. Perhaps this business is, as our friends at Gatorade would describe life, "a sport."

Those Who Expect Miracles, Perform Miracles

Let me introduce you to Maxwell Maltz, author of the outstanding book, *Psycho-Cybernetics*. Maltz was also a nationally renowned plastic surgeon. Maltz believed that if he could correct an individual's deformities, he could improve his or her self-image. I saw the before and after pictures of his subjects. Maltz's work was absolutely amazing; he was extremely successful in correcting physical defects. However, the effects of the wonderful metamorphoses were not exactly what he had expected. You see, although he was able to transform "ugly ducklings" into physically attractive individuals, his patients still perceived themselves as unattractive. Maltz found that he also needed to change the data constraints that had been programmed into their brains during the years when they had been disfigured. The good news is that once these individuals were taught to act and think positively, their whole personalities changed. They became more confident, outgoing, and assertive. And do you know what? They also started to perceive themselves as being attractive and appealing. Isn't that great?

Once, I was in India for the International Boxing Championships. After the tournament, I went with a number of the other American boxers to a little café to get something to eat. When a woman passed the window of the café, all the non-Americans jumped up and ran to the door to watch her as she walked by. Being a red-blooded American man, I too ran to the door to see what had caused such a stir. I figured the woman had to be a cross between Cory Everson and Vanessa Williams. What I saw was the exact opposite. I kept telling myself, "This can't be the woman who is getting these guys all excited." But it was. You see, in India, a stout woman is most desirable. These guys had been taught their whole lives that portly women were attractive. And that woman was just strutting her stuff like Madonna at a rock concert. She knew she was good-looking. Obviously, "fine" is in the mind. If she believes it, then that's what she is.

As I've mentioned, the magic of believing in yourself applies not only to physical appearance, but to every aspect of human behavior. All of our feelings, behaviors, and even our abilities are consistent with our conditioning and/or programming. In short, we tend to "act like" the type of person we believe ourselves to be.

It shouldn't surprise you then, when I tell you that the most consistent finding in sports-related research is the direct

> **There is a direct relationship between self-confidence and success.**

relationship between self-confidence and success. Self-confidence is the key to success in the financial business, too, but it takes education and time to develop the skills. It's not unlike being a world-class chess player. It takes time, but, above all, you have to want it. For the professional broker or money manager, once you gain this self-confidence, developing new business takes on a different light. You become an educator rather than a prospector. People gravitate to you because they intuitively feel this newfound confidence. What once might have looked like a failing career becomes, instead, a flourishing business. You learn to love your business again. Such a turnaround is within your reach—you just have to want it. This business I talk about also applies to individual investors. If you want to take control of your finances and the responsibilities that go with it, you must have confidence in your abilities to do so. As with professionals in this business, unless you have confidence you are doomed to failure.

Confident athletes, athletes who believe in themselves, not only love to compete, but they also love to compete against the best. Athletes who are confident believe they can do anything and often do. Stockbrokers are the same, without a doubt. I have seen them during my twenty-nine years in the business. We have the benefit at my firm of talking to hundreds of brokers each day, and it's clear that those who are confident about their abilities do the best. I've talked many times about my brokerage days in the 1970s. The confidence I had in my abilities to invest my clients' money was at an all-time low. I knew I didn't have a plan of attack. It was just hit or miss. We received mounds of paper from New York each day and were expected to pick out a few stocks and sell them. So I began prospecting people who made less money than I did, because I knew my level of knowledge in the investing world was above theirs. Well, it was, but only barely. I knew enough to be dangerous. It's hard to see yourself as a winner if half the recommendations you make go south. It's confidence that determines a winner or loser in this business, or in any business for that matter.

Winning in the brokerage business happens when you have a solid plan that you stick to and that earns your clients a return that exceeds inflation and taxes. Their nest eggs continue to grow on a real basis, without taking undue risk. Anything else is fantasy. But it takes time to develop this plan of attack. It takes study to understand how to fit the fundamental side of the equation, what to buy, with the technical side, when to buy, and how to manage both sides. Once an investor has taken the time to learn how to meld the two schools of thought, fundamentals and technicals, his confidence will shoot through the roof. He will then see himself as a winner, and his new self-image will translate into consistent positive returns in his portfolio. For the professional, customers will gravitate to him like bees to honey. This confidence gained by learning is contagious and there is no stopping it.

Brokers, individual investors, and athletes with this type of confidence never quit. They constantly see themselves as winners, never losers. They focus totally on the positive. They expect miracles and, consequently, they make miracles happen. I have met many professionals in this business who have just thrown in the towel. In the end, they could not stand to consistently lose

> **Confident individuals act positively, talk positively, and never minimize their abilities.**

their clients' money. Such an outcome weighed heavily on them and, in turn, affected their personal lives. I have seen brokers who were about to get out of the business until they learned how to use the Point & Figure Method and then miraculously turned their business around. Some of you who are reading this now are those people and you know exactly what I mean.

Confident individuals act positively, talk positively, and never minimize their abilities. When athletes, brokers, and individual investors think negatively, they generally fail; conversely, those who think positively usually succeed. Just look around you. How many people do you know think negatively and how many think positively? You might be astonished if you count them. Don't forget, negativity is contagious, too. Stay away from people who are always negative, and hang with the positive ones. It will rub off. It's that simple. What an athlete, broker, or investor thinks and/or believes is critical to his performance. World-class athletes and brokers believe that they are among the very best. Consequently, they act and perform as if they are the best.

Obviously, the way your brain has been programmed will go a long way toward determining how successful you'll be in athletics, finance, and in life. If you've been conditioned to believe you can, there's an excellent chance that you will. But, if you've been conditioned to believe you can't, you most likely won't. How many times do you read or hear in advertisements on TV that you "can't time the market?" You can't add any value in that respect so don't even try. Mostly it's the media types who are just saying, "I have not been able to do it, so you undoubtedly can't either," or the mutual funds that want their investors to stay fully invested at all times, so they can continue charging management fees. I can't tell you how many investors I have talked with who have succumbed to that mantra: You can't, so why try? Well, anyone who has followed the Point & Figure method with us over the last seventeen years knows that you CAN! Don't let anyone tell you you can't be world-class. All it takes is a desire to attain that height. Don't let yourself end up on that bus looking out the window, watching others reach greatness.

Here's something else you need to know. There literally is magic in believing. Even if you have a poor self-image at this point in time, you are not doomed to failure in business, investing, or life in general. You can change. You can become a positive, self-assured individual.

This Is Going to Hurt Me More Than It Hurts You

Have you ever heard those words? "This is going to hurt me more than it hurts you." The last time I heard that, I was eight or nine years old and the following elements, in no particular order, were involved: police, spray paint, Dad, leather belt, property damage. I don't know about you, but whenever I hear those words today I think about discipline and punishment and also about how wrong it is to spray paint the KISS logo on the front doors of a middle school. (It was 1976 and they were a popular band. Give me a break!) Looking back, I'm sure it was much more painful for my dad to discipline me than it was for me to be on the receiving end of his punishment. And not just out of his embarrassment that my vandalism involved KISS instead of, say, the Rolling Stones or Led Zeppelin.

I was reminded again of the familiar phrase about *hurt* in a recent discussion with an investor. He was upset about taking profits in some positions only to see that the stock continued higher. His reasoning for taking profits was that the Point & Figure indicators had rallied into overbought territory and some of the short-term indicators had begun to reverse down to O's. While we never advise "anticipating the anticipators," there is certainly nothing wrong with, and even something very disciplined about, taking some profits.

In this particular case, the investor had taken about one-third of their positions off the table and moved closer to 66 percent invested. Only 20/20 hindsight would have been able to determine if that was prudent or fearful, but the point is that it was predetermined in his accounts that once the short-term indicators moved above 70 percent and back to defense, the account would move one-third back to cash. The working theory for the accounts was that raising cash into strength, as the short-term indicators were high and reversing down, would build ammunition for putting more money to work on pullbacks. That makes sense. This is going to hurt me more than it hurts you.

Sure enough, although the investor followed the game plan to a tee, he was none too pleased to see the market continue to rally nicely over the next couple of weeks. It's human nature that we want to take all the gains and leave all the losses. However, what the investor was forgetting was that he was still two-thirds invested. The best possible situation for him was for the market to continue to move up. When trimming positions and adjusting for risk in the portfolio, human nature has us forgetting the tenets of the strategy. I like to think about it like car insurance. Every six months you pay the insurance company a premium to make you whole in case you have an accident. At the end of the six months we don't say to ourselves, "Shucks, I can't believe I didn't get in an accident. I wanted to put myself through a potentially dangerous situation, the anguish in get-

> **The disciplined approach is often the most difficult approach.**

ting the car fixed and procuring a rental car, and the ability to 'stick it' to the insurance company." What we say is, "Whew, made it through another six months without an accident or a ticket. Wonderful."

The point here is that the disciplined approach is often the most difficult approach. That's why they call it *discipline* instead of *fun*. There's nothing much fun about discipline as it happens. The reward comes much later. That's why it's difficult: the pleasure is delayed. And that's why it's right.

Patience Is Waiting Without Worrying

As I drive home from work each day, I pass by a Methodist church that has some of the best sayings on their marquee outside. One Monday when I drove by, they had just put up another gem; "Patience is waiting without worrying." You know, that is so accurate. Do you remember that, as a kid, it was so hard to have patience sometimes. Christmas is a prime example. It seems that at Christmastime many a child's patience is tested. Children eagerly await the arrival of Christmas morning to see whether Santa has visited their house. Using the old "You'd better be good or Santa will bring you coal and switches" seems to be a very effective disciplinary tool for parents to start using around Thanksgiving. Better yet, "You'd better be good or Santa won't visit you." Up until that magical morning, there is a mystery that surrounds the event. Children read stories that keep their imaginations vivid. Will Santa come? Will Rudolph be guiding the sleigh? How will Santa get down the chimney? What will Santa bring? Will Santa like the cookies we left for him? All of these unknowns make it hard for children to find patience during the Christmas season.

> **Fear of the unknown causes worry, but patience comes when you know how to navigate the future.**

Of course, as we all grow older, we learn how the magic of Christmas morning with presents under the tree is created. Then those mysteries about Christmas morning disappear and are replaced by patience in awaiting its arrival. On the other hand, a new set of mysteries surrounds the holidays and can sometimes make adults lose patience. Will Uncle Bob be late for dinner again? Will Aunt Louise bring that awful fruitcake and insist that everyone have a slice? How will Grandpa Joe react to Cousin Sue's new boyfriend, the one with orange hair and three nose rings? Again, the unknown elements cause worry to overtake patience.

I think the same elements come into play in the stock market. Fear of the unknown causes worry, but patience comes when you know how to navigate the future. Think back to the technology bubble. Many investors did not take defensive action when the technology indicators reversed down in 2000. Then, at the beginning of 2001, these stocks experienced strong rallies, but the trends of many stocks never changed to positive. The fear gripping most investors at that point was "What if these stocks continue to rally and I miss it?" To that I answer, "Patience is waiting without worrying."

In the markets, patience is often a difficult thing to have. With a definitive game plan for investing, however, one can have patience. For us, the Point & Figure methodology is the perfect game plan because it is based upon the laws of supply and demand. When supply begins to take control of a stock, we see sell signals on the trend chart that are indicative of further price declines. As supply creeps into a sector, the whole group of stocks begins to experience a downward move in price. When that balance between supply and demand changes, we know to change our market posture. We also know that the sector has a low probability of having sustainable rallies. Therefore, by having a game plan, you have some rules that help guide your investment posture. A plan allows us to be patient and rest assured that we will have strong indications when things change. As things change, we change. We never predict their change. What is, is.

No one ever has a crystal ball to know exactly how something will work out. The best anyone can do is to take the information available at that moment and make the best possible decision. At Dorsey, Wright we always make the right decision. Sometimes those decisions have bad outcomes, and then we go into damage control mode. Risk management techniques are the most important techniques to learn when investing. Many investors have been faced with a situation where they are unsure of selling a position. On the one hand, they want to stop the bleeding; on the other hand, they are paralyzed by the fear, "I might sell at the bottom." If the charts are telling you that supply is still in control, selling is the right decision and you don't have to fret. Not all decisions will be right, but if you stick to your indicators and game plan, you will be right more often than you are wrong. Only with a solid game plan built upon the irrefutable laws of supply and demand can you have patience for the next opportunity without worrying that you will miss it.

Success Is in the Doing, Not the Getting

In America, and in the brokerage business in particular, most people equate wealth with success. If you have a lot of money, it is assumed that you are successful in life. In fact, most Americans think there is a linear relationship between money and success. In the finance or sales world, those who are referred to as "big producers" are assumed to be successful. I know that was drilled into me when I started out as a broker. I know people in this industry who are quite wealthy and considered to be grand successes. I guess the big question is "Can money buy happiness?" We do know that it can buy a lot more happiness than poverty can. Money sure can buy lots of material things. Pearl Bailey may have summed it up best when she said, "Honey, I been poor, and I been rich. And let me tell you, rich is much better." She is probably right, but I can tell you this: money isn't everything.

Have you ever read the book *Quiet Desperation: The Truth About Successful Men* by Jan Halper? I think it is out of print. You might have to find it at a rare book Web site. The book focuses on men who had power, money, and wealth, all the trappings of success. Interestingly, few of these men were happy and most of them were miserable. Why? Well, as Harper points out, having power and affluence is not the same thing as having success. These guys had all the money in the world, but they had lost sight of things essential for health and happiness. They had become addicted to making money and, in so doing, had become enslaved to wealth and all its accoutrements. In the process, they lost themselves. Instead of gaining time and freedom from their affluence, they lost those very things. (Sound a little like the dot-com craze and the 24/7 work schedules?) Instead of gaining the respect, esteem, and admiration that wealth can command, they forfeited it. In short, those men cheated themselves out of the other things that make life so enriching and worthwhile. Think for a second. I'm sure you know someone who is wealthy, yet somehow not happy. I know that you can name at least a handful of movie stars or athletes who fit this persona.

If money isn't the key to success, then what is? That is not an easy question to answer, but I believe Wynn Davis has the right notion. He says, "Success means doing the best we can with what we have. Success is in the doing, not the getting; in the trying, not the triumph." We become successful when we push our hearts and souls to the furthest capacities. When you go home at night, can you say you gave it all you had today? Even if you did not do one dollar of production, did you give it your all? With respect to your investing, are you aware of the technical attributes you should have with each position? Do you have a solid, logical, and organized plan of what to do if things go wrong and what to do if they go right? Is the plan

> # The key to riches is enriching the lives of others.

well-founded and in the best interest of the account? Or do you come into work each day thinking of how many sales you have to make to keep your numbers up? I used to do that when I was a new broker.

Probably the most important part of becoming successful is to come to work *prepared* each and every day. This is not an easy task. It's kind of like going to school prepared each day. Those of you who did, more than likely did very well. Those of you who did not (like me), probably did very poorly. Goals that have nothing to do with money breed success. Money can never be your goal. The key to riches is enriching the lives of others. In this way you will be enriched in the end. This has been the policy and goal of Dorsey, Wright from the beginning and it has not changed one iota for seventeen years. It permeates every employee's mind at DWA. It's our way of life! It's our brand! It doesn't matter if you are closing a big business contract, competing at the World Championships, or just playing Old Maid. If you do your very best, you will never be disappointed, no matter what the outcome. As Davis says, "Success is not in the getting, it's in the doing."

I'm sure you have heard of Mickey Mantle. When I was a little boy, he was everyone's idol. He was a baseball phenomenon. Mantle had everything you could want in a baseball player: world-class running speed, an arm like a rocket-launcher, incredible hand-eye coordination, and awesome bat velocity. Best yet, he was a switch-hitter, and, man, could he hit! Not only did he hit for average, he also hit for power from both sides of the plate. Add to that his incredible ability to field balls and you have, what we call in stock technical attributes, a "five-for-fiver." He was inducted into the Baseball Hall of Fame and ranked one of the top twenty-five baseball players of all time. What an accomplishment! He had it all: money, fame, and prestige. But do you know what he said right before he died? In essence he said, "I'm ashamed of my career. God gave me all of these wonderful physical gifts and I abused them. I drank, I stayed out nights, and I never practiced hard. I have so many regrets, because I know that if I had done my best, I could have been so much better. Maybe I could have been the best of all time . . . Look at my career and see what you shouldn't do, not what you should do."

Right to his dying day, Mantle felt that he could never make amends for the life he felt he had wasted; that was his cross to bear. This brilliantly talented man, who had the world in his hands, threw it all away because he was too foolish to realize that true happiness comes from accomplishment, not amusement. There will always be that "what if" that lingers about Mantle. What if he had applied himself; what contributions could he have made to his sport and his fellow man? I, too, experienced many of the negative things that Mantle had experienced. I'm glad I recognized my mistakes early enough to make the necessary changes.

You know, in all the years that I've been in sports, one athlete stands out in my mind as being the greatest. You've probably never heard of him. His name is Kenny Hall and his sport is boxing. He's never won a World Championship, a National Championship, or even a Regional Championship, but in my mind he's the greatest athlete I've ever come in contact with. Why do I feel that way? Mainly because Kenny got the very most out of what God gave him. Every time he went out, he performed at an optimum level, both physically and mentally. He took every moment to the very limit, every moment. Best yet, he performed the same way in practice. He pushed himself to the ultimate point of possible development. Now that's "greatness."

I don't care how important you are or how much money you have, there is no worse feeling than walking away from something knowing you could have done it better, wondering *what if?* When you don't push yourself to the limit, you limit yourself. Robert Louis Stevenson said, "To be what we are, and to become what we are capable of becoming, is the only end of life." I see it in the gym every day. Not everyone is a National Champ or a World Champ, but they are all life's champs because they come back day in and day out and achieve the most they can achieve with the bodies God gave them. Some are there for power, some for muscle development, and others for fitness, but they are all champions. Every last one of them. They not only devote the day to their profession, whether blue collar or white collar; they also devote their time after work to becoming all they can be in their chosen sport.

No matter what profession you have chosen, there is no doubt in my mind that success is attainable for you. But it

> **Success means getting your hands dirty, struggling a little, suffering a little, and working a little.**

comes with a price. Success means getting your hands dirty, struggling a little, suffering a little, and working a little. It means taking responsibility for choosing and defining your own life. It means being the very best you can be. Are you ready to become the Seal team of your chosen profession? I hope so, because that possibility is there for the taking.

Dorsey, Wright & Associates

Left to Right, Bottom Row: Justin Knight, Tammy DeRosier, Tom Dorsey, Susan Morrison, Steve Raymond; Left to Right, Top Row: Nancy Emig, Paul Keeton, Kevin Depew, Jay Ball, and Watson Wright.

Dorsey, Wright & Associates (DWA) is an independent and privately owned registered investment advisory firm whose business includes two areas—investment research services for broker-dealers, large institutions, and individual investors around the world, and professional management of equity portfolios for investors.

The two principals of the firm, Thomas J. Dorsey and Watson H. Wright, founded the firm in 1987. Since inception, the firm has grown to fifteen employees in three offices: the home office in Richmond, Virginia, DWA Money Management in Pasadena, California, and DWA Consulting based in Nashville, Tennessee.

Tom Dorsey is the author of *Point & Figure Charting: The Essential Application for Forecasting and Tracking Market Prices* (1st and 2nd editions), *Thriving as a Stockbroker in the 21st Century*, and *Tom Dorsey's Trading Tips: A Playbook for Stock Market Success*, along with other DWA analysts. *Point & Figure Charting* has been translated into German, Polish, two dialects of Chinese, Hindu, and most recently, Japanese.

The DWA team speaks all over the world on the Point & Figure methodology, risk management of equity and fixed income portfolios, and motivation. Tom Dorsey is a regular guest on Fox's "Cavuto, on Business" and "Bulls and Bears" programs, and the DWA analysts appear on numerous financial radio and TV venues, such as CNBC's "Taking Stock" and Bloomberg TV.

Tom Dorsey is a recipient of the Wharton School of Finance Securities Industry Association's "Distinguished Speaker Award." He was also named Alumni of the Year 2000 for Virginia Commonwealth University as well as the Citizens Community Award from Governor Charles Robb. Dorsey, Wright & Associates received runner-up awards in the Ernst & Young Entrepreneur of the Year Award 1999 and runner-up Best Small Business of Richmond, Virginia, in 1999. DWA was also honored with the Business Leadership Award from Virginia Military Institute.

Tom Dorsey is an AAU Dead Lift World Record Holder, an American Record Holder, and he holds state records in power lifting for his age group.

Dr. Judd Biasiotto

Dr. Judd Biasiotto is the president of World Class Enterprises, a sports fitness corporation. He has worked as a sports psychologist with numerous amateur and professional athletes and sports teams, including the Kansas City Royals, the Pittsburgh Pirates, and the Cincinnati Reds. He is the author of thirty-seven books and more than six hundred articles and is considered one of the top sports writers in America. One of his most recent books, *The Search for Greatness*, received a sports Emmy from the American Sports and Science Academy. He is a feature writer for six national magazines, including *Muscle and Fitness, Shape*, and *Natural Physique*. Dr. Biasiotto was recently selected to the International Platform Association, a nonprofit organization that honors the best speakers and orators in the world.

In addition to his professional achievements, Dr. Biasiotto also has the rare distinction of being a world-class power lifter and bodybuilder. He has set 101 state records, forty-seven region records, twenty-three American records, sixteen national records, and four world records. In 1987, he was ranked as the fourth-best power lifter of all time by *Powerlifting USA*. In the year 2000 he was named one of the top fifty lifters of the millennium by *Powerlifting USA*. His best lifts, at a body weight of 132 pounds, include a bench press of 319 pounds and dead lift of 551 pounds. In 1988 Dr. Biasiotto shocked the sports world by squatting an incredible 603 pounds, at a body weight of 130 pounds. That lift, which exceeded the previous ADFPA world record by over eighty pounds, is considered one of the most prolific feats of strength in the history of the sport of power lifting. Just as extraordinary, in 2003, Dr. Biasiotto became the oldest man to win the WNPC national and world open bodybuilding championships.

LEARN RISK MANAGEMENT ON YOUR TIME SCHEDULE

Dorsey Wright Global Online University

A step ahead in the world of investors.

Start learning the steps to managing risk . . . at your own pace.

- Classes 2–3 weeks in length.
- Class lectures via streaming video.
- Lively Web-based class discussions.
- Instruction by top analysts.
- Case studies and exams to test your knowledge.